YOUR KNOWLEDGE HAS VALUE

Competence in Schools in Tanzania. Influence of the Competence of the Principal on the Students' Academic Performance in Secondary Schools

Chelestino Mofuga

Bibliographic information published by the German National Library:

The German National Library lists this publication in the National Bibliography; detailed bibliographic data are available on the Internet at http://dnb.dnb.de.

ISBN: 9783346256294
This book is also available as an ebook.

© GRIN Publishing GmbH
Nymphenburger Straße 86
80636 München

Print and binding: Books on Demand GmbH, Norderstedt, Germany
Printed on acid-free paper from responsible sources.

The present work has been carefully prepared. Nevertheless, authors and publishers do not incur liability for the correctness of information, notes, links and advice as well as any printing errors.

GRIN web shop: https://www.grin.com/document/924976

INFLUENCE OF COMPETENCE ATTRIBUTES OF HEAD OF SCHOOLS, ON THE STUDENT ACADEMIC PERFORMANCE IN SELECTED SECONDARY SCHOOLS IN TANZANIA. A CASE STUDY OF MBULU DISTRICT

Author: Dr Chelestino Simbalimile Mofuga

Abstract

This study assessed the influence of the competence attribute of the educational leaders on the student academic performance in the secondary schools. Explanatory cross-sectional survey design with a concurrent mixed approach using quantitative and qualitative data were employed. A total of 202 teachers used to provide evidence on heads of schools competence in influencing students' academic performance using questionnaires, in-depth interview and focus group discussion. The collected data were analyzed using SPSS version 23 for quantitative data, and thematic analysis for qualitative data. Significant relationship between competence and students' academic performance was revealed. The study concluded that competence attribute significantly influence positively the students' academic performance Therefore, the study recommends the government to allocate enough funds for professional development for the aspirant of head of schools and review educational policy on the training and development of teachers before and after appointment into headship post.

KEY WORDS: competence, leadership, Academic performance.

Index

ABBREVIATIONS:

HoS   Head of school

FGDs   Focused group discussion

SPSS   Statistical Package for Social Scientists

RCC   Regional consultative meetings

NECTA   National Examination Council of Tanzania

SD   Standard Deviation

SDA   Strongly Disagree

DA   Disagree

NT   Neither disagrees nor agrees

AG   Agree

SA   Strongly agree

1. Introduction

The context of quality of education provided in secondary schools worldwide in the 21st century depends much on the competence of teachers in their schools. The educational stakeholders are enforced with not only quality of school buildings, facilities, school environment and other services provided in the school, but the quality of knowledge and skills obtained by students. And there is no miracle to gain knowledge based competence without professional competence of teachers. Elvira et al (2017) argue that in an increasingly competitive environment to provide better education. Education institutions should focus on improving the students' academic performance. This performance embodied in student grade which then support the graduated student who search for jobs. Besides improving the mental attitude, educational institutions should also improve cognitive abilities. One of the important factors which can contribute in improving cognitive abilities is teacher professional competencies. Teacher should have a wide and deep knowledge regarding the course or subject they teach. They also possess practical experiences so that their lesson becomes more attractive and understood by students.

The quality of an educational institutions or secondary school can be seen from the quality of graduates it produces. One of the key indicators which show the quality of education is the grade point average (GPA). The cumulative GPA is the result of the overall study of the student over certain time. One important aspect which can affect student academic performance is the teacher. Teachers regarded as the most imperative school based factor that influences student's achievement level (Muzenda, 2013). They can help to change the student attitude and help them to accomplish better performance. In order to do so teacher must have suitable competencies. Ganyaupfu(2013) also mention that teacher competence has significant influence on the student performance. According to Akiri (2009) teacher competence in learning process will drive and help the student to achieve better performance. Sultan and Shafi(2014) supports the ideas regarding the relations of teacher competence and academic performance. On the other hand Yoon et al (2007) , found that teacher who receive substantial professional development can boost their student achievement.

Elvira et al (2017) state competence as a range of knowledge and behavior which must be possessed by teacher or lecturer in order to do their duties. Teacher competence includes their knowledge, skills, and behavior which help or enhance the capabilities of teacher to educate, teach, guide, direct, train and evaluate the student. Ones' competence should include communication skills, ability to learn, conduct social interaction, problem solving skills, working with ICT or other support tools (Zeravikova et al 2015). It is evident that professional competencies are closely related to the performance of a job. Competence presupposes the personal competency of teacher and the knowledge and skills which become necessary as a result the job (Liakopoulou, 2011).

Amuche and Saleh (2013) found that in North Central Geo-political zone of Nigeria and secondary school principals were not professionally competent to carry out school administration and planning duties. Akiri (2013) disclosed that in public secondary schools in Delta State, Nigeria, the good academic performance of students was associated with qualified teachers. This also was confirmed by Long *et al*. (2016) who revealed that performance of students was linked with teachers' competencies in terms of creativity, knowledge, communication, discipline, and adequate students' preparation. Mustamin and Yasin (2012) study focused on the competence of school principals based on Ministry of Education Malaysia; Florida Department of Education, and Ministry of National Education Indonesia. Base on the purpose of this study, documentary review was conducted by adapting methods of concept mapping. The study identified that competency is the ability, knowledge, attitudes, and skills of doing the job effectively and efficiently. The study further pointed out that school principals need to have these attribute as are essential for school success. School leaders with competency attribute indirectly impact students academic performance by influencing teachers contentment in teaching activities through motivating them, sharing the vision and mission of the schools. Also, competent school leaders place learners at the centre with a collaborative approach which ensure vision, mindsets, culture, and climate of the school is in favour of both teachers and students in teaching and learning process.

Molefe (2010) conducted a study to develop a generally accepted performance measurement dimension framework for lecturers at universities. The research purpose was to investigate the performance measurement dimensions for lecturers at selected universities in countries South Africa, USA, UK, Australia and Nigeria. Universities were selected on the basis of their academic reputation; being the best in their respective countries or continents. A quantitative research approach was adopted using data collected through a questionnaire. Main findings confirmed that a lecturer's performance can be measured using seven competency dimensions; subject knowledge, testing (assessment) procedures, student-teacher relations, subject relevance, organisational skills, communication skills, and utility of assignments. Moreover, the dimensions were tested, and attracted a Cronbach Alpha reliability coefficient of above 0.70.

A research in South Africa by Muzenda (2013) analysed the effect of lecturers' competences on students' academic performance among higher education and training students. A structured questionnaire was used to gather data on 115 students selected using simple random sampling procedure. The scale reliability Cronbach's alpha of 0.822and the sampling adequacy Keiser-Meyer-Olkin of 0.769; with a total declared variance of 66.519 percent were obtained from the analysis. Four hypotheses were tested using Stepwise regression approach. Results indicate that dimensions of lecturer competence; lecturer teaching skills, subject knowledge, and lecturer attitude and lecturer attendance have a positive significant influence on students' academic performances.

In addition, Goolamally and Ahmad, (2014) in their quantitative study identify and affirm the conceptual framework and attributes of school leaders (principals) needed to achieve leadership sustainability and school excellence in Malaysia, found that head of schools needs five attributes in order to excel in school leadership and make a school excellent: integrity, inspirational, competency, forward-looking and self-efficacy. Thus, competent, which has the sub-attributes of task competency, action-oriented and sociability as well as emotional and spiritual competency, was found to influence school achievement in Malaysia. This study focused on leadership attributes of the head of schools and ignored to assess the influence of attributes to student academic performance.

On the contrary, Prasetio et al. (2017) assessed lecturers' professional competency and students' academic performance in Indonesia higher education in an increasingly competitive environment. This study examined the relation between lecturers' professional competency of lecturer has an impact on students' academic performances in higher education. The findings show that the professional competency does not have a significantly relation with students' academic performance. The detail discussion provided with new insights of various factors which might relate to the performance. However, this study assessed the influence of headmasters' competency on academic performance of secondary school students. Accordingly, the findings from Wamala and Seruwagi (2013) in Uganda suggest that teachers' competency alone may not directly translate into better students' academic performance.

In similar view, Abbasi & Mir (2012) conducted a study in Pakistan to assess the influence of teachers' competency or ability, students' work ethics and institution environment on students' academic performance. The results indicated that, independently; teacher abilities, student's work ethics, and institutional environment did not have significant influence on student performance. But, simultaneously these factors; have a strong significant effect on student academic performance. Moreover, Kosgey et al. (2013) and as Bonney et al. (2015) both also support the non-significant result. Studies showed that even if the quality of teachers was high in terms of their academic and professional qualification it did not drive the performance of the students. Thus, there was no significant relation between competence and student performance. Moreover, Lee and Yuan (2013) manifested that the leadership styles of the supervisors significantly have direct effect on effectiveness of the organizations.

Makario (2014) investigated the influence of head teachers' management of facilities on pupils' performance in Kenya Certificate of Primary Education (KCPE) in Nairobi County, Kenya. The study employed descriptive survey design. The sample size was 123 selected using a simple random sampling method while for the schools, head teachers, senior teachers and accounts' clerks, purposive sampling method was utilized. Descriptive statistics and distribution techniques were used to analyze the data. The main findings were: high level of adequacy of the school facilities, competence of head teachers, and documentation of facilities, gender of the head teachers, and very adequate delegation of responsibilities to staff in management of facilities had the best pupils' performance in KCPE. The study concluded that the tested variables influenced the strategies employed by head teachers to effectively manage school facilities and enhance 'pupils' performance in KCPE.

Ndyali (2013) attempted to analyse the roles of the head of schools in the achievement of student's academic performance in community secondary schools in Mbeya Urban. Both quantitative; survey and qualitative; in-depth interview and focused group discussion were conducted. The results of the study revealed that the school heads are surrounded by many challenges which make the school management to be unbearable. Their roles had been hampered by unfriendly working situations in which schools operate under shortage of teachers, facilities, funds and lack of commitment among stakeholders. The study concludes that the students' poor academic performance in the context of the roles of school heads prevailing in community secondary schools is a result of an educational system that produces predetermined poor results.

Day and Sammons (2014) investigated associations between the principals' role and performance of primary and secondary schools in England. The study revealed that the the principle has important role of improving the academic performance. Moreover, according to Robinson (2007), studies conducted on the qualitative research on the leadership attributes and the link to student outcomes were found to be only 24 published researches between 1985 to 2006 in Australia. Also, Mulford (2005), conducted a study to determine the contribution of leadership attributes on the student academic performance for five years between 2001 and 2005. The study found only 44 published academic journal articles. Thus, it can be postulated that there is inadequate research on the field of leadership attributes of head of schools and its influence on student academic performance today. Hence those studies show the empirical research gap of lacking of literature in leadership attributes and academic performance. Moreover, based on the review of literature, it was suggested that there was little research on the influence of school leaders' competency attributes and student's academic performance. Therefore, this study was imperative as it examined the head of the school's leadership competence attribute on student's academic performance in Tanzania.

1.1 Main Objectives

To assess the influence of competency attributes of Head of schools on the students' academic performance in selected secondary schools.

1.2 Specific Objectives

1. To assess the influence of work competency of Head of schools on the student academic performance in selected secondary schools
2. To assess the influence of emotional competency of Head of schools on the student academic performance in selected secondary schools
3. To asssess the influence of spiritual competency of Head of schools on the student academic performance in selected secondary schools
4. To assess the influence of practical competency of Head of schools on the student academic performance in selected secondary schools

7

2. Methodology

In this study, both quantitative and qualitative data were analyzed but separately. The aim was to draw valid inferences about what has been analysed and to avoid any spurious relationships. The quantitative data were subjected to computer software, Statistical Package for Social Science (SPSS) Version 23. This software enabled the researcher to record variables, select cases and to compute new variables. Through the use of SPSS software, the researcher determined descriptive such as means, frequencies, and percentages as well as cross-tabulation or chi-square and model goodness of fit test between independent and dependent variables. This enabled the researcher to confirm the existence of the relationship, direction of relation and strength of the relationship between the dependent variables and independent variables. Also, qualitative data were organized prior to being edited, coded or grouped, tabulated or compiled by the researcher. As such triangulation was employed in data analysis. In the course of presenting the findings, quantitative data were concretized by qualitative data obtained through interviews, focus groups, observations and information obtained from documents.

2.1 Qualitative Analysis

Qualitative analysis is not guided by universal rules (Rao and Woolcock, 2003), is a very fluid process that is highly dependent on the evaluator and the context of the study. The literature describes the process of qualitative data analysis as involving: transformation of raw data by identifying, examining, preparing and organising masses of raw textual data collected, reducing, mapping, exploring, describing patterns and trends and categorizing the data into themes in relation to the research problem, questions and conceptual framework of the study by using a process of coding, and condensing the codes in order to interpret them and provide their underlying meanings; and finally displaying the data in an organized, compressed assortment of information that allows verified conclusions to be made (Patton, 2002: 41; Braun and Clarke, 2006; 2013; Ngulube, 2015).

Accordingly, the qualitative data analysis in this study, identified, prepared, organized, coded and categorized the qualitative data into patterns and themes in relation to research questions and conceptual framework and the results were used to complement quantitative findings. This section provides a loosely structured guide for the steps the researcher undertook when analyzing qualitative data.

Thematic data analysis was used to analyze interview transcripts and relevant documents in order to identify patterns of recurring themes and sub-themes in line with the research questions. Content analysis is the most common form of analysis in qualitative research as it emphasizes in pinpointing, examining, and recording patterns (or "themes") within data (Lacey and Luff, 2001; Creswell *et al.*, 2004). Both conceptual and relational analyses were applied in content analysis. In the conceptual analysis, important concepts (themes) were established and analyzed based on the frequency of occurrence during discussions and its trend in a text or communications. On the other hand, relational analysis groups together the related themes and or patterns of data. Themes are important to the description of a phenomenon and are associated with a specific research question. This study adopted the six procedures of thematic analysis proposed by Lacey and Luff (2001) (see Table 2.1)

2.2 Quantitative data analysis

Data collected through structured questionnaires were summarized and coded. Statistical package for social sciences (SPSS) version 23.0 and Microsoft excel 2007 were employed for data analysis and figure construction respectively. This software is user-friendly in analyzing and presenting statistical data (Landau and Everitt, 2004). The quantitative analysis was both descriptive and inferential statistics. Descriptive statistics such as chi-square, correlation coefficients; Phi, Cramer's V and Kendall's tau-b, frequency, and percentage distribution and measures of central tendency; mean and standard deviation, were calculated for all four objectives of the study. The descriptive data were analyzed to describe and gain an understanding of various sample characteristics (Hair *et al.*, 2007).

3. Findings and Discussion

In this section, the results on the influence of competency attribute of head of schools on the student academic performance in selected secondary schools in Mbulu district. The level of competency attribute of heads of schools in school leadership was measured by 11 statements or items of interest as indicated in Table 3.1. The section answers the question; How to determine the competency attributes of the head of schools on the student academic performance in selected secondary schools in Mbulu district?

Descriptive statistics such as frequency distribution and measures of central tendency (mean and standard deviations) of every item for all participants and of all 11 items for every 202 participants were quantified to measure the distribution and variability of school heads' competency attribute from the mean, on average. Also, inferential statistics were performed to examine the extent to which competency attributes of school heads determine the students' academic performance specifically in Mbulu district and Tanzania.

Frequency distribution of competency indicators was calculated. Table 3.1 summarizes frequencies and percentages distribution of the 11 items of competency attribute to measure the extent of competency attribute on school leadership and its impact on students' academic performance in Mbulu district. The results show that all 11 qualities (items) of competency attribute were found to be possessed by heads of schools because they were important in school leadership and hence students' academic performance in Mbulu districts.

9

Competency of the head of school is crucial as it defines what a leader does and how does it. For that reason, a school head must build school capacity through an effective leadership style to influence student achievement through teachers. To enable this school head must have or be able to develop the capacity and competency to work with school staffs to focus on curriculum, instruction and student learning outcomes.

The competency attribute has three sub-attributes, namely, work competency, emotional competency and spiritual competency (Goolamally and Ahmad, 2014). In one hand, items such as quality giving direction; ability to focus in the future; and professionalism fall under work competency. On the other hand, items Heads of schools being convincing when developing a vision; facilitation and negotiation; organizational climate and culture; and managing change are categorized as emotional competency. Also, contribution to the community and profession fall under spiritual competency.

In this study, descriptive results (Table 3.1) of HoS competency indicate that the item which says heads of schools adhere to professionalism scored the highest frequency of 78.70% (sum of 33.70% strongly disagreed and 45.00% disagreed). This means that professionalism is the most important attribute of inspirational leadership in HoS of Mbulu district. It also means that heads of schools in Mbulu district abide highly to professionalism. They follow and enforce rules, guidelines, procedures and the code of conduct for the head of schools and teachers as a teacher him/herself. Also, another item which scored the highest sand considered highly essential for competent HoS was; HoS contribute to the profession and community (78.70%).

Furthermore, Table (3.1) show that most of the surveyed teachers reported that HoS were professional and thus contributed to the development of the professionalism of themselves and their staffs in general. Supplementary findings showed that HoS emphasized professionalism among staffs by enforcing adherence to professional moral principles (ethics), codes of conduct, professional culture, and values. These included prohibiting staff-student or student-student sexual relationship or affair, prohibiting students from having affair with anyone in the community or beyond, and to make sure affairs among teachers does not affect work by reminding them to be faithful to their relationships.

Furthermore, teachers in the focus group in Mbulu district had also a lot to comment about the competency of heads of schools. The FGD participant among the teachers said passionately:
> "The head of my school does understand the education system and how it works, he is a good manager and adheres to professionalism... he has a good and keen interest in students' and teachers' welfare... a facilitator and a manager...our school's form four results of last year were impressive though below national target"

Similarly, another teacher happily added that:

> "Our head of school is keen, smart and organized... she focuses in the future through her fascinating visions and gives quality directions which contributes to community and profession"

Moreover, the second-highest scores were recorded for 2nd and 5th items in Table 3.1; the ability to focus in the future (76.60%) and capacity to manage communication and relationships with clients (76.60%). Similarly, the item that asks if the head of schools possess the ability to give quality direction (76.20%) was the third important attribute of inspirational. Additionally, during semi-structured interviews, the key informants on the question of competency attribute, they said that among other things head of school competence is essential for improving students' academic performance. The key informants, the head of the secondary school section at the district level had these to say:

> "Although most of heads of schools had never attended leadership courses. I can say for sure that they are competent...they give quality directions, manage change, they are good negotiators as they possess high convincing power and fascinating visions, charismatic and professional"

Moreover, another key informant, an education inspectorate passionately had this to say:

> "I agree that heads of schools are competent in doing what they are required to do... very cooperative, have fascinating visions of the future... they are responsible for students' and teachers' performance. However, some heads of school are inexperienced and incompetent thus hamper school and students' academic performance..."

Likewise, one informant, ward education coordinator enthusiastically narrated that:

> "Yes, it is true; the heads of schools are competent though they lack some technical skills essential for school leadership..."

Moreover, HoS were found to be visionary. The study disclosed (Table 3.1) that HoS have the ability to see and focus on the future for the school advancement in academic as well as non-academic achievements. It was further found out that HoS were visionary as they could see opportunities and possessed the ability to tap the opportunities today for the future school benefits. Besides, HoS were seen to be able to develop realistic projections and predictions of the schools and secondary education in general. Some of HoS could explain the future of education so eloquently and convince their staffs and other people. In a semi-structured interview, participants corroborated the findings explaining that some HoS were experienced enough to anticipate the future of our education.

In the case of HoS competency in giving worth direction, the study found that most of the respondents said that HoS possessed that quality. It was further revealed that in applying and putting into effect the quality of giving meaningful directives; HoS usually directs staffs to accomplish their work in a manner that acceptable, directs teachers on how best they can perform their daily activities such as teaching, management of students' discipline, and extracurricular activities and directs students to behave themselves so that they can graduate or pass with flying colours. Thus, HoS is the director and manager of all the school activities. Also, in a semi-structured interview, key informants had a similar outlook. All key informants favoured that HoS had been giving important directions to the staffs based on the directives of the policy, by-laws, and guidelines. In addition, in case of facilitation and negotiation competency, HoS were found to apply this quality through negotiating with other schools on matters of academic such as conducting joint examinations for form two and four students, and other related issues such as sports and games, students' discipline management, resource mobilisation and exchanging of ideas and expertise among teachers and non-teaching staffs. Also, the HoS was found to be responsible with the task of seeking or requesting help or donation from well-wishers such as organization, community, and individuals. A key informant added that, as a leader, HoS is expected to foster the relationships and keep those relationships for as long as it can take because school performance depends on them. In Mbulu this is not a problem anymore as many schools have a good relationship with the surrounding community.

In the case of leadership skills and behaviour, the study established that most of the heads of schools possessed leadership skills and behaved themselves as leaders. In this head of schools were found to treat all teachers, non-teaching staffs and students equally/justly, ensure peace and harmony at school, listen to and act on complaints brought to him/her by staffs or students or community members as well as neighbouring organizations and treat them equally. Additionally, the study revealed that HoS were competent and could respond to people regardless of their status, manage organizational culture, instil to new teachers and students the school values, and control and monitor school teaching and learning environment to ensure improved students' performance. The survey results were confirmed by key informants.

Therefore, the general view of the study based on the descriptive findings, depict that HoS had demonstrated a high degree of competency. It was revealed that they treat all the teachers and staffs equally with respect and cooperation. Heads of schools involve teachers and no-teaching staffs in the decision-making process such as teaching allocation, conflict resolution, extracurricular activities and disciplining staffs and students. With this level of integrity Mbulu secondary school education is expected to rise soon.

Mean and standard deviations of 11 items of competency attribute of school leadership were computed. The results (Table 3.2) depicted that most of the items had little dispersion and variability around the mean of the data set, on average. So, the values in the statistical data set are close to the mean of a sample population. This signifies consistency of data and thus reliability and validity of data. However, the items which showed high variability around the mean of data set they just reflect a large amount of variation in the group that is being studied (Al-Saleh and Yousif, 2009:196; Rumsey, 2016). This study considered a group of individuals who had a variety of features.

4. Conclusion

The heads of schools were found to highly apply their competency qualities in their leadership to encourage the teaching and learning process with the ultimate goal of improving students' academic performance. The study found that competency of HoS significantly influences the students' academic performance. It was found that absence of competency attribute in school leadership decreases students' academic performance because HoS with no competence were less likely (fewer odds) to report a pass grade of their students compared to HoS with competency attribute.

Consequently, encouraging HoS to acquire more competencies in school leadership is imperative. Since most HoS enter this position without adequate skill and training, so to impart them with the skills, they need to be trained in leadership to get instilled with leadership attributes such as competency. Thus, funds for training HoS and other teachers should be allocated and the government should review the educational policy especially the training and development policy so that they can be trained before and after appointment to headship.

5. Tables and Figures

In this section, the researcher presents results for the assessment of the influence of competence attribute of the heads of schools on the students' academic performance in selected secondary schools in Mbulu district. Table 2.1, 3.1 and 3.2 summarises frequencies and percentages distribution of the 11 items of competence to show the extent of application of competence attribute on school leadership and its impact on students' academic performance in Mbulu district as discussed above (section 3.0 Findings and discussion).

Table 2.1: Thematic Analysis of Secondary Schools Teachers' FGD in Mbulu DC

Criteria for appointing HOS	School leadership	Improve school leadership	Impact of school leadership	Education delivery	Student's academic achievements
-Experiences -Accountability -Hard work -Committed educational qualification -Competency -Leadership skills -Discipline/honest -Supervision -Talents	-Able to delegate -Motivate positive attitudes -Accountable -Participatory -Conflict resolution -Transparent -Teamwork	-Training of HOS -Training of DHOS -Training of teachers/seminars -Budget for training -Provide residential houses and transport -Head of schools must be; • Competent • Accountable • committed • motivate	-motivate staff -encourage students -improve school supervision -teamwork and collaboration -Improve knowledge and skills -Attract experienced teachers -Improve school effectiveness -Improve academic achievements	-Competency of teachers and students -Integrity -Inspirational attributes -Visionary leadership -Teaching environment -Learning environment	-Improved student academic performance -Improved school attendance -Improved student discipline -Improved pass marks in science subjects -Improved student motivation Improved teachers motivation

Source: **Field Data, 2019**

Table 3.1: Frequency Distribution of Competency Indicators (N=202)

	Indicator	SDA N(%)	DA N(%)	NT N(%)	AG N(%)	SA N(%)
1	Quality giving direction	07(03.50)	19(09.40)	22(10.90)	94(46.50)	60(29.70)
2	Ability focusing on the future	04(02.00)	16(07.90)	25(12.40)	84(41.60)	73(36.10)
3	Being convincing when developing a vision	06(03.00)	06(03.00)	41(20.30)	86(42.60)	63(31.20)
4	Gripping vision be able to express values and strategies	05(02.50)	15(07.40)	36(17.80)	84(41.60)	62(30.70)
5	Communication and relationship management	03(01.50)	12(05.90)	32(15.80)	78(38.60)	77(38.10)
6	Facilitation and negotiation	05(02.50)	12(05.90)	41(20.30)	83(41.10)	61(30.20)
7	Leadership skills and behaviour	06(03.00)	31(15.30)	16(07.90)	75(37.10)	74(36.60)
8	Organization climate and culture	04(02.00)	09(04.50)	45(22.30)	108(53.50)	36(17.80)
9	Managing change	04(02.00)	14(06.90)	41(20.30)	91(45.00)	52(25.70)
10	Professionalism	07(03.50)	11(05.40)	25(12.40)	91(45.00)	68(33.70)
11	Contribution to the community and profession	06(03.00)	08(04.00)	29(14.40)	93(46.00)	66(32.70)

Source: Field Data, 2019

Table 3.2: Mean and Std Deviation of Competency Attribute Items (N=202)

S/N	Item/Statement	Mean	Std. Deviation	N
1	Quality giving direction	3.90	1.043	202
2	Ability to focusing on the future	4.02	.992	202
3	Being convincing when developing a vision	3.96	.951	202
4	Gripping vision be able to express values and strategies	3.91	1.001	202
5	Communication and relationship management	4.06	.955	202
6	Facilitation and negotiation	3.91	.980	202
7	Leadership skills and behaviour	3.89	1.150	202
8	Control Organization climate and culture	3.81	.851	202
9	Managing changes	3.86	.949	202
10	Professionalism	4.00	.998	202
11	Contribution to the community and profession	4.01	.949	202

Source: Field Data, 2019

6. Disclosure of Conflict of Interest

The findings revealed in this study is only merely research study, does not reflect the weakness of individual person, rather the education institutions particularly the selected secondary schools for the purpose of improving the student academic performance. And the data collected were highly observed confidentialities and were used for academic purposes only. Should any person relate the information's obtained here into the report, with any person or group of people, should not be treated as crime since all ethical procedures regarding academics were followed thoroughly well?

7. Acknowledgement

The support and assistance of my supervisors' Dr Cosmas B.M. Haule and Dr Joseph J. Magali were invaluable to the work. I truly, appreciate the encouragement and support of my supervisors, their contributions and encouragement to learning activities was quite valuable as they guided me without getting tired. I also thank my staff workers in my District commissioner office particularly to support my work whenever they were required either through fulfilling my duties or academic contributions. I would like to thank too, the Manyara regional Commissioner Hon. Alexander Pastory Mnyeti for his encouragement and support of permission whenever required to travel for academic purposes. I really enjoyed learning and growing alongside of each of them, their humour and remarkable insight made every learning interesting and engaging.

8. References

Aaker, D.A., Kumar, V., and Day, G.S. (2001). *Marketing research*. New York, USA: John Wiley and Sons Inc. Page 751

Abdullah et al (2012). The need to explore emotional intelligence (EI) skills amongst Malaysian public librarians. Proceedings of international business information management (IBIM) May 2012, INstabul ISSN 978-0-98214897-6

Abubakar, U. (2018). The difference between education and academics (Blog post). Accessed from https://tutors.com.ng/2018/08/02/the-difference-between-education-and-academics/html

Ache Health Care. (2018). *Health care leader's alliance and the college of healthy executives' competencies assessment tool*. USA. Author.

Adam, J. and Kamuzora, F. (2008). *Research methods for business and social studies*. Morogoro, Tanzania: Mzumbe Book Project.

Adebayo, F.A. (2009). Parents' preference for private secondary schools in Nigeria. Kamla-Raj 2009. *International Journal of Education Science, 1(1), 1-6*

Adeleye, J.O. (2017). Pragmatism and its implications on teaching and learning in Nigerian schools. *Research Highlights in Education and Science*, Page 2-6

Adeyemi, O. T. (2013). Principal's leadership styles and student academic performance in secondary schools in Ekiti State, Nigeria. *International Journal of Academic Research in Progressive Education and Development*. 2(1), 187-198

Afeli, (2017). *Regional workshop on national learning assessment systems in Sub-Saharan Africa: Knowledge sharing and needs assessment*. Paper presented at the UNESCO and TALENT Workshop on National Learning Assessment Systems in Dakar, Senegal from 6th to 8th December, 2017.

Ahmed, J.U. (2010). Documentary research method: New dimensions. *Indus Journal of Management and Social Sciences*, 4(1), 1-14

Ahmed, S. (2009). Statistical methods for sample surveys (140.640): Introduction to sampling method (Lecture). University of John Hopkins.

Ahmet, AVCI. (2016). Effect of leadership styles of school principals on organizational citizenship behaviours. *Educational Research and Reviews*, 11(11), 1008-1024

17

Ajayi, V.O. (2017). *Primary sources of data and secondary sources of data; Distinguish between primary sources of data and secondary sources of data.* Benue State University, Makurdi. Faculty of Education Department of Curriculum And Teaching

Akaranga, S.I. and Makau, B.K. (2016). Ethical considerations and their applications to research: a Case of the University of Nairobi. *Journal of Educational Policy and Entrepreneurial Research,* 3(12), 1-91.

Akiri, (2017). Lecturer's professional competency and student academic performance, in Indonesia Higher Education. *International Journal of Human Resources Studies,* 7 (1).

Akiri, A.A. (2013). Effects of teachers' effectiveness on students' academic performance in public secondary schools; Delta State – Nigeria. *Journal of Educational and Social Research,* 3(3)

Aline, I. and Ramkumar, S. (2018). Leaders are not born, they are made. *International Journal of Applied Research,* 4(5), 94-96

Al-Karasneh, S. and Jubran, A. (2013). Classroom leadership and creativity: A study of social studies and islamic education teachers in Jordan. *Creative Education,* 4(10)

Alkarni, A. (2015). Problems which may challenge the ability of secondary school head teachers in the City of Tabuk to lead their schools professionally. *ARECLS,* 11, 55-74.

Allen, N., Grigsby, B. and Peters, M.L. (2015). Does leadership matter? Examining the relationship among transformational leadership, school climate, and student achievement. *NCPEA International Journal of Educational Leadership Preparation,* 10(2)

Allport, G. W., and Odbert, H. S. (1936). Trait names. A psycho-lexical study. *Psychological monographs,* 47, pp 211.

Almalki, S. (2016). Integrating quantitative and qualitative data in mixed methods research— challenges and benefits. *Journal of Education and Learning;* 5(3)

Al-Saleh, M.F. and Yousif, A.E. (2009). Properties of the Standard Deviation that are rarely mentioned in classrooms. *Austrian Journal of Statistics,* 38(3), 193–202

Alvaro, C., and Maria, G. (2017). *Does school leadership affect student academic achievement?* Fundació Jaume Bofill, Ivàlua.

Amuche, C.I. and Saleh, D.A. (2013). Principals managerial competence asa correlate of students' academic performance in Ecwa secondary schools in North Central Nigeria. *Journal of Education and Practice,* 4(4).

Annie, W., Howard, W.S. and Mildred, M. (1996). Achievement and ability tests: Definition of the domain. Educational Measurement 2, University Press of America, pages 2–5.

Appoline, A.T. (2015). *Motivational strategies used by principals in the management of schools. The Case of some selected secondary schools in the Fako division of the Southwest region of Cameroon.* Master's Thesis in Education, Department of Education, University of Jyvaskyla.

Ardichvili, A., Dag, K.N. and Manderscheid, S. (2016). Leadership development: Current and emerging models and practices. *Advances in Developing Human Resources*, 18(3), 275-285.

Arshad M., Zaidi, S.M.I.H and Mahmood K. (2015). Self-Esteem and academic performance among university students. *Journal of Education and Practice*, 6(1), 156-162

Asimaki A., and Vergidis K. D. (2013). Detecting the gender dimension of the choice of the teaching profession prior to the economic crisis and imf (international monetary fund) memorandum in Greece: A case study. *International Educational Studies*, 6(4), 140–153.

Avery, G.C. (2004) *Understanding leadership: Paradigms and cases.* London: Sage.

Awiti, F. S. (2013). *Management strategies of teachers turn over in Ilala municipal.* A Dissertation Submitted for Partial Fulfilment of the Requirements for the Award of the Degree of Masters of Science in Human Resources Management of Mzumbe University.

Ayeni, A. J. (2005). *The effect of principals' leadership styles on motivation of teachers for job performance in secondary schools in Akure South local government.* A Dissertation Submitted to the Department of Educational Administration and Planning for Partial Fulfilment of Award of Masters Art in Education of Obafemi Awolowo University, Ile-Ife.

Azaliwa, E.A and Casmir, A. (2016). A comparative study of teachers' motivation on work performance in selected public and private secondary schools in Kilimanjaro region, Tanzania. *International Journal of Education and Research. 4(6)*, 583-600

Babajani, J. (2008). The analysis theatrical and legal basis of 2008 budgeting new approach of view accountability, *Hesabdar*, 194, 4-5

Babajani, J. (2010). Challenges of public sector financial reporting. *Hesabras*, 48, 96-97

Bahta, S.T. and Bauer, S. (2007). *Analysis of the determinants of market participation within the South African small-scale livestock sector.* Tropentag, October 9-11, 2007, Witzenhausen:

Utilisation of diversity in land use systems: Sustainable and organic approaches to meet human needs. Tropentag Paper.

Bailey, K.D. (1982). *Methods of social research* (2nd Ed.). New York: Free Press. 553 p

Balihar, S. (2007). Qualitative research methods: documentary research (Blog post). Accessed from http://uk.geocities.com/balihar_sanghera/qrmdocumentaryresearch.html

Balliro, M.J. (2018). *The new sincerity in American literature.* A dissertation submitted in partial fulfilment of the requirements for the Degree of Doctor of Philosophy in English of University of Rhode Island

Bandura, A. (1997). *Self-efficacy: The exercise of control.* New York: W.H Freeman and Company

Baron, R.M., and d Kenny, D.A. (1986). The moderator–mediator variable distinction in social psychological research: Conceptual, strategic, and statistical considerations. *Journal of Personality and Social Psychology,* Volume 51(6), 1173–1182

Barth, R.S. (2009). *Improve schools from within: Teachers, parents, and principles can make a difference.* San Francisco, CA: Jossey-Bas.

Bass B. M., (1990). *Bass and Stogdills handbook of leadership. theory research and managerial application.* New York: Free Press.

Baum, D.R. and Riley, I. (2018). The relative effectiveness of private and public schools: evidence from Kenya. *An International Journal of Research, Policy and Practice.*

Baxter, and Jack, (2008). Qualitative case study methodology: Study design and implementation for novice researchers. *The Qualitative Report,* 1(4), 554-559.

Bedi, A. S., and Garg, A. (2000). The Effectiveness of private versus public schools: The C\case of Indonesia. *Journal of Development Economics,* 61(2), 463-494.

Begna, T.N. (2017). Public schools and private schools in Ethiopia: Partners in national development? *International Journal of Humanities Social Sciences and Education, 4(2), 100-111*

Bennel, P. and Mukyanuzi, F. (2005). *Is there a teacher motivation crisis in Tanzania?* Research Report Fund. Dar es Salaam: HR-Consult.

Bennell, P. (2004). *Teacher motivation and incentives in Sub -Saharan Africa and Asia.* Brighton: Knowledge and Skills for Development

Bennis, W. G., and Naus, B. (2003). *Leaders: The strategies for taking charge.* New York: Harper and Row.

Bernardo, A. B. I., Ganotice, F.A. and King, R.B. (2014). Motivation gap and achievement gap between public and private high schools in the Philippines. *The Asia-Pacific Education Researcher*, 24(4).

Bill, M. (2008). *The leadership challenge in improving learning in schools*. Australia: Australia Council for Educational Research,

Black, P.J., Woodworth, M. and Porter, S. (2014). The big bad wolf? The relation between the dark triad and the interpersonal assessment of vulnerability. *Personality and Individual Differences*, 67, 52-56.

Blanche, M. T., Durrheim, K. and Painter, D. (2006). *Research in practice: Applied methods for the social sciences*. Juta and Company Ltd.

Bleiklie, I. and Michelsen, S. (2013). Comparing higher education policies in Europe: Structures and reform outputs in eight countries', *Higher Education*, 65, 113–133.

Bleiklie, I., Enders, J., Lepori, B. and C. Musselin (2011). New public management, network governance and the university as a changing professional organization', in T. Christensen and P. Laegreid (eds) *The Ashgate Research Companion to New Public Management*, (pp. 161–176) (Farnham: Ashgate).

Bloor, M., Frankland, J., Thomas, M., and Robson, K. (2001). *Focus groups in social research*. London, Thousand Oaks -CA: Sage Publications Inc.

Bolat O.İ, Bolat T, and Seymen O.A (2009). Güçlendirici lider davranışları ve örgütsel vatandaşlık davranışı arasındaki ilişkinin sosyal mübadele kuramından hareketle incelenmesi. Balıkesir Üniversitesi Sosyal Bilimler Enstitüsü Dergisi 12(21), 215-239.

Boniface, R., (2016). *Teachers' retention in Tanzanian remote secondary schools: Exploring perceived challenges and support*. Doctoral dissertation, Department of Education, Linnaeus University, Sweden.

Bowen, G. A. (2009). Document analysis as a qualitative research method. *Qualitative Research Journal*, 9(2), 27-40. doi:10.3316/QRJ0902027

Braun, V. and Clarke, V. (2006) Using thematic analysis in psychology. *Qualitative Research in Psychology*, 3 (2), 77-101.

Burns, N., and Grove, S. K. (2003). *The practice of Nursing Research: Conduct, critique and utilization*. Philadelphia: W. Saunders.

21

Byabato,S., and Kisamo, K. (2014). Implementation of school based continuous assessment in Tanzania ordinary secondary schools and its implications on the quality of education. *Developing Country Studies*, 4(6)

Campanelli, P. (2008). Testing survey questions. In E.D. De Leeuw, J.J. Hox, and D.A. Dillman (Eds), *International Handbook of Survey Methodology*, New York: Lawrence Erlbaum Associates

Cardoso, S., Carvalho, T. and Santiago, R. (2011). From students to consumers: Reflections on the marketisation of Portuguese higher education', *European Journal of Education*, 46(2), 271-284.

Caspar, R., Peytcheva, E., Yan, Y., Lee, S., Liu, M. and Hu, M. (2016). Pretesting Cross-cultural survey guidelines. CC56

Ceil, C., and Sykes, J. (2012). *Women in leadership*. New York: Social Science Electronic Publishing Inc. Retrieved November 28, 2015, from http://ssrn.com/abstract=2051415

Cerit, Y. (2009). The effects of servant leadership behaviours of school principals on teachers' job satisfaction. *Educational Management Administration and Leadership* 37(5), 600–623

Chaudhary, A.K. and Israel, G.D. (2014). The Savvy survey #8: Pilot testing and pretesting questionnaires. IFAS extension, University of Florida

Cheng, Y.C and Townsend, T. (2000). Educational change and development in the Asian Pacific region: trends and issues, In T. Townsend and Y.C. Cheng (Eds). *Educational change and development in the Asia-Pacific region: Challenges for the future,* Rotterdam: Swets and Zeitlinger.

Cherrington, David J. and J. Owen, Cherrington (1993). Understanding honesty. *Internal Auditor, pp* 29-35.

Cherry, K. (2016). *What is the trait theory of leadership?* Retrieved from https://www.verywell.com/what-is-the-trait-theory-of-leadership-2795322

Cherry, K. (2019). *How extroversion in personality influences behaviour.* Accessed from https://www.verywellmind.com/what-is-extroversion-2795994

Cho, J., and Trent, A. (2006). Validity in qualitative research revisited. *Qualitative Research,* 6(3), 319-340.

Chrzanowska, J. (2002). *Interviewing groups and individuals in qualitative market research* (Vol. 2). London: Sage. 176 p

Churchil, G.A. and Iacobucci, D. (2005). Marketing research: Methodological foundation (9th Ed.). USA: Thomson South-Western

Churchill, G. A. (1996). *Basic marketing research (3rd Ed.),* Fort Worth, TX: The Dryden Press

Clarke, J., and Wood, D. (2001). New public management and development: The case of public service reform in Tanzania and Uganda. In McCourt, W., and Minongue, M., (Eds.), *the Internationalization of public management: Reinventing the Third World State.* Cheltenham, Edward Elgar.

Clarke, V., and Braun, V. (2013). Teaching thematic analysis: Overcoming challenges and developing strategies for effective learning. *Psychologist, 26*(2), 120-123.

Cohen, L., Manion, L., and Marrison, K. (2007). *Research methods in education (6th edition).* London: Routledge Taylor and Francis group. 638 p.

Commission Malaysia.

Conger J.A., and Kanungo R.N, (1987). Charismatic leadership in organization perceived behavioural –attributes and their measurement. *A Journal of Organizational Behavioural,* 15, 439-452.

Conroy, R.M. (2016). The RCSI sample size handbook: A rough guide

Cortina, J.M. (1993). What is coefficient Alpha? An examination of theory and applications. *Journal of Applied Psychology,* 78(1), 98-104

Creswell, J. W. (2007). *Qualitative inquiry and research design: Choosing among five approaches (2nd ed.).* Thousand Oaks, CA, US: Sage

Creswell, J. W. (2014). *Research design: Qualitative, quantitative, and mixed methods approaches.* Sage. 342 p.

Creswell, J. W., and Plano Clark, V. L. (2011). *Designing and conducting mixed methods research* (2nd ed.). London: Sage.

Creswell, J. W., Fetters, M. D. and Ivankova, N. V. (2004). Designing a Mixed methods study in primary care. *The Annals of Family Medicine, 2*(1), 7-12.

Creswell, J.W. (2009) *Research design: qualitative, quantitative, and mixed methods approaches* (3rd Ed.). Thousand Oaks, CA: Sage.

Crossman, A., and Harris, P. (2006). Job satisfaction of secondary school teachers. *Educational Management and Leadership, 34(1),* 29-46.

Crow, G. (2001). School leader preparation: A short review of the knowledge base. National College for School Leadership. Available at http://www.ncsl.org.uk/mediastore/image2/randd-gary-crow-paper.pdf

Cuthill, M. (2002). Exploratory research: citizen participation, local government and sustainable development in Australia. *Sustainable Development,* 10, 79-89.

Dang, V. H. (2015). A mixed method approach enabling the triangulation technique: A case study in Vietnam. *World Journal of Social Science,* (2)2

Daniel, R. (2003). *The Role of school leadership on student achievement.* Luxemburg, Italy.

Gbollie, C. and Keamu, H.P. (2017). Student academic performance: The role of motivation, strategies, and perceived factors hindering Liberian junior and senior high school students learning. *Education Research International,* Volume 2017, Article ID 1789084, 11 pages

Hidalgo (2002) .Integrity retrieved from http//www.webweever.com/integrity.htm

Mohd Najib(2009), I Malaysia concept can earn the country respect, retrieved from: http//www.1malaysia.com.org/index

Polit D.F and Beck C.T (2010). Generalization in quantitative and qualitative research: Myths and strategies. International journal of nursing studies, 47(11) 1451-1453

Risik et al 920110, A cross-cultural examination of the endorsement of ethical leadership, journal of Business Ethics 63(4), 345-359

Salmon D. And Rickby C(2012), City of one. A quantitative study examining the participation of young people in care in a theatre and music initiative, children and society.

Shek D.(2012), Evaluation of a positive youth development program based on the repertory and test. The scientific journal world journal 2012, 1-12.

Sidek (2009), Public services people first, perform